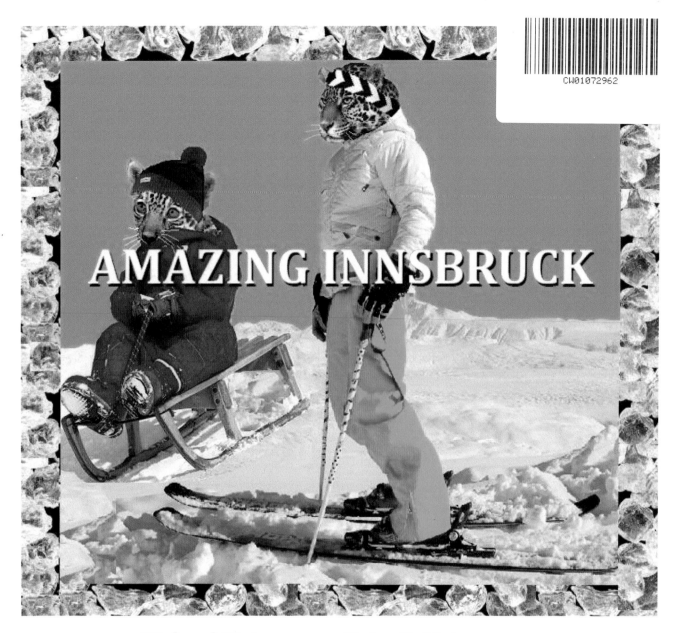

AMAZING INNSBRUCK

Richard Matevosyan, Naira R. Matevosyan

Copyright © 2013, L'Auteur Librairie
ISBN: 978-1494300753 / CreateSpace, Inc.

" We are in Innsbrücke," roared father jaguar, "the capital of the federal district of Tirol – western Austria, a destination so perfect for the winter sports! You must appreciate that Innsbruck has hosted three Olympics: in 1964, 1976, and 2012."

" It's snowing quite profusely!" sighed the cub from the tomb of a slop.

"Trust me... there is nothing more appealing than the feeling of skiing down the

slopes with the rush of wind against your face as the sunlight permeates the winter sky, resonating a glow that showcases the snow-coated mountain peaks perched in the distance!" thundered father jaguar. "Ah, I am deep with the Alps! It is an 8-inches of fresh cutter and I want nothing, absolutely nothing, but to give a try to my first run of the day... Actually it's the first for the season. Hopefully, my muscles still know how to do this!"

"When the skiing sport was invented?" meowed the cub.

"The oldest evidence of skiing is found in Norway and Sweden. The earliest

primitive carvings circa 5000 B.C. – depicting a skier with one pole – are found in the

Norland region of Norway. The first primitive ski dates back to 4,500–2,500 B.C. and

is found in a peat bog in Hoting, Sweden. The first recreational ski club was formed in

1861, in Australia. There are two types of skiing: *Alpine*, and *Nordic*. The first one includes the *Freestyle, Surfing, Biathlon* and *Hillskiing*, and the second type includes *Telemarketer, Ski-fountaining, Cross-country-skiing, Dry-slop-racing, Sectoring, Ski-touring, Ski-jumping*, and *Ski-flying*. Now, I gonna try the ski-flying in the Alps! Ah...! It's good for my soul!"

"Be careful dad, take it easy!" screamed baby jaguar.

After the very first tantalizing ride, the jaguar found himself hanging from a treetop and started crying for help in German: *"Hilfe, Hilfe!"*

After indulging an adrenaline rush and crash, at noon our tourists in rosettes walked down the bridge, crossing the river Inn.

"To me, Innsbruck is more than a place for winter sports," noticed the cub. "There are so many affable traditions we have to explore in this Alpine city. One of those is the bell making tradition. The word's most grand bells are made in here."

"Indeed," agreed the jaguar. "Innsbruck is famous for its bell-making art and

history. But it is also renown for a percussion of a hot music performed by a gadget!"

"And ... a place, where drinking schnapps is in itself an Olympic event!"

"I have always thought of Innsbruck as an exclusive winter-resort destination," purred father jaguar, "but imagine my surprise when we arrived. It is a CITY - a truly gorgeous one!"

"It's also a hub for youth creation and education," noticed the cub. "Founded in 1669, the *Universität Innsbruck* is one of the oldest Universities in Austria and one of the best with its 4,000 staff and 27,000 students."

"We're now in the historical *Altstadt von Innsbrücke* (The Old Town), a 500-year old picturesque place with mesmerizing buildings raised since 1500s – retaining their beauty and flair. People residing here are rich. The buildings are unique with their arch-ways and bay windows. This architecture is a smart accommodation for the scarce sunlight. Gasthof is the main street; this is where the Emperor used to travel in his horse-driven carriage."

"I admire the colors of each building," meowed the cub.

"They have been in the same shape from 1500s to present. These buildings possess a monumental significance and the residents are forbidden to make color or design changes. Finally! We reached the hottest ticket," roared the jaguar, "the landmark of Innsbruck called *Das Goldene Dachl* (The Golden Roof),"

"Is it truly made from gold?" asked the cub.

"I doubt... Currently a museum, it was built in 1500 by the order of Emperor Maximilian I to mark his wedding to Bianca Maria Sforza. The roof was decorated with 2,738 fire-gilded copper tiles. The Emperor and his wife used the balcony to observe festivals and tournaments. The entire oriel is decorated in sculpted reliefs and mural paintings."

"Overall, the whole Altstadt is very compact and it takes only a few hours to explore it inside and out – even to go for grocery shopping," suggested the cub.

"Let's buy meet jerky from this store, *Spezialitäten aus der Stiftgasse*," roared the hyper-oxygenated and hungry jaguar.

"Look! I found a tiny boutique speck-store," noticed the cub.

"It's small, but it has a vast assortment of speck (bacon) and smoked veal - the local meat product. Just name it!" the jaguar dressed his whiskers.

"Grüß Gott!" greeted them the store manager. "My store is designed to feed the hikers. Innsbruck is literally the front-floor step to the Alps. Look at the mountain Katha! Before climbing the mountains you need to be prepared to maintain your strength on the top. There, in the fresh Alpine air, you get hungry fast. You will need to take with you a substantial food, like heavy salami or speck and schnapps. So please,

make your selection! And... the schnapps store is the next to mine."

"I've noticed that everyone here offers me schnapps," purred the jaguar entering the neighboring store.

"It is the most important thing here, advised the store manager. "If you want to stay healthy, you have to drink schnapps! But you must drink it once a day with a meal, drink in small amounts and very slowly. Schnapps is a strong liquor (32-56% alcohol) distilled from different fruits. Österreich is a schnapps country! My store offers a local schnapps called *Obstler* or *Obstbrand.* These spirits are actually *eaux de vie.* We have a broad collection of homemade schnapps, distilled from apple, pear, cherries, and plum mixed together. Tastes like the almond! If you want to get familiar with the vast variety of prominent brands, like *Pater Noster, Absinthe Mata Hari,* or *Wiener Blut,* there is a Schnapps Museum and Supermarket in Vienna."

"Very nice, I"ll take a bottle. *Danke Schon! Auf wiedersehen!"* the tourist paid 19 Euro for a bottle and left the store.

"Let's dine at this pub," suggested the cub.

"We have to choose between the local *Carpaccio* or *Beef Tartare*," said father jaguar. "The first one is a typical Austrian Schnitzel: a filet mignon cut in gauzily slices and dressed with balsamic olive oil.

The second is from a rough ground meet seasoned with capers of onions, Dijon mustard, and served with toast and butter. Delightful! All entries or dishes are served in the wooden plates."

"What shall we have for the dessert?" asked the cub.

"If you want to make it Austrian, I suggest you order Saga Torte or green-apple strudel," suggested the jaguar.

"Now it's time to explore the authentic Tirolean lifestyle in a village outside Innsbruck. Let's take a horse and make a round," meowed the cub.

"Yeah," sighed father jaguar, "life hasn't changed much here over 500 years. See that barn connected to the house ...! This is because cows, horses, geese, sheep and chicken – all were held in the same building to create heat for the family lived in...

This was a survival trick to safe on heating. Clever, ha!"

"It might be smelling quite differently..." mentioned the cub.

"Oh yes, but I'd rather prefer to stay warm," explained the jaguar.

"The houses are so beautiful," noticed the cub, "we must take a slow pace ride to enjoy this incredible Alpine charm. Take a look at the balconies, flower-baskets, decorative paintings which make this village seem

untouchable over the centuries."

"I agree. And there are around 25 vacation houses in this village offering bed and breakfast with Tirolean fun," noticed the jaguar.

 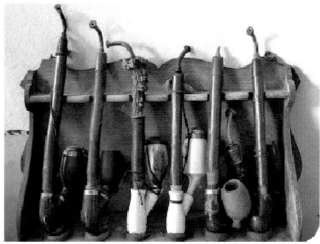

"This spectacular village, stationed at the mountains, must be attracting many tourists," meowed the cub.

"Of course it does! Tirol has both: the great land and the location. With

its 3,000-meter high 700 mountains an endless line of jagged snow-capped peaks, fast-flowing rivers, pretty villages, lush green meadows, onion-domed churches, it expands from western Austria to northern Italy. The province Tirol consists of the

nine districts of which eight belong to Austria. Seven make up North Tirol, which

borders the Austrian provinces of Salzburg and Vorarlberg, as well as Germany, Italy and Switzerland. Also known as East Tirol, the Lienz district is the number eight. The ninth area, South Tirol, lies across the Italian border."

"Why is it divided in such a way?" asked the cub.

"A larger area, covering three districts, was known as Tirol since the 14th century, a part of the Austrian-Hungarian Empire. At the end of the World War I Italian troops penetrated into South Tirol. With the dissolution of the empire Italy annexed the southern part of Tirol pursuant to the Treaty of Saint-Germain in 1919.

Trends to Italianate the South Tirol since 1920s were ineffective. The South Tirol's Italian speakers are pretty very much in the minority. By and large, the two communities get on well, though with separate churches, schools and political clans.

Oops! We are running late. Our next stop is the crystal factory," said the jaguar looking at the itinerary in his i-phone. "There, the world's famous crystal makers will show us how it feels to be inside their mysterious product!"

"This is quite different than anything else in Innsbruck!" sighed the cub.

"Indeed. The large crystal eyes on the man's face on terrace already hints what it is it about!"

"Swarovski!" meowed the cub, "the guru of the contemporary crystal art."

"Inside this hill, which is only 15 minutes from the village Wattens, you will

open a crystal world! You think that this might be a typical museum where the

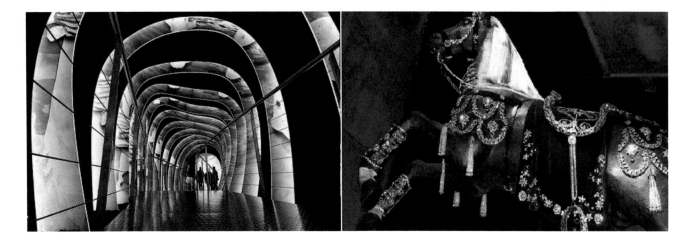

contemporary artists display their products... Nope, what you will see here may surprise you: a vast collection the famous paintings from Salvador Dali, Andy Warhol, or Jasek Yerka -- transformed into the multi-dimensional crystal theatre," thundered the jaguar.

"Look at Salvador Dali's *'Soft Watches'* in a freeze glass!" exclaimed the cub.

"This fellow is one of us," noticed the jaguar, "a diamond jaguar in its full repertoire, sculptured by Swarovski A.G!"

"In the middle of the museum seats the largest-cut crystal in the world: 300,000 carats!" the cub approached it.

"Even the walls here are filled with the sparkling crystals. Now I understand why this place is called *'Crystal worlds'* - in plural. One world is real and tangible, the other one is a surreal crystal fantasy!" reflected the jaguar.

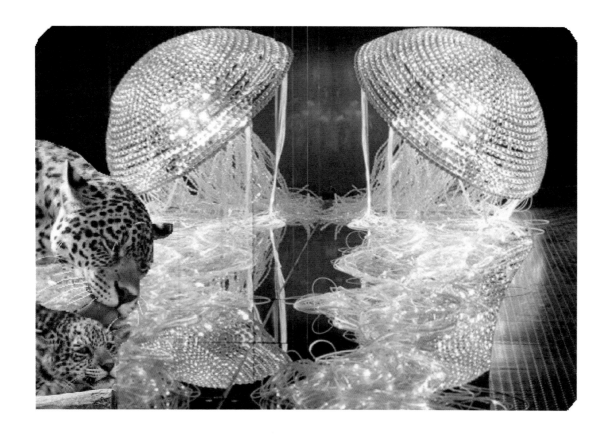

"This is the Crystal Dome. A strange atmosphere inside, the music, and the change of colors. Wow!" roared the jaguar. "Now we are in the Crystal Maze room established by Daniel Swarovski. It is a virtual world where you chase after yourself. It is so unexpected. When you come here you hope to sea vases, animals, or ornaments. Instead, your senses are treated by this exhibit which includes even the planet Earth in silver and crystal, with a perfect display of all its goodness! This place causes you to spontaneously react to sights or smells. I do not really know

27

how to describe what I feel now."

"That is the reason we call it a surreal world..." advised the little cub. "Here, you never get the point and you never have to."

"That's the point!" thundered father jaguar.

"Let's move to the reality," suggested the cub. "I want to see New Innsbruck."

"While the Old Innsbrücke was established in 1500s, the New City has emerged in 1700s. If you are planning to spend the whole day in New Innsbruck, you might have to purchase an Innsbruck Card. It allows you a free access to the major attractions, museums, parks, and unlimited public transportation.

This is a very easy city to get around and perhaps you will be walking for most of the time, but it worth to have this card. Our hotel is ten minutes from this place; so let's walk!"

"What's the name of our hotel?" asked the cub.

"*Schwarzer Adler!*" replied the jaguar. "It means Black Eagle."

"I see the eagle sign on the entrance," meowed the cub.

"The double-headed black eagle was the symbol of the Austrian-Hungarian Empire. Today, this hotel is a romantic site with a close look to the Alps. It is also a

very historical building, because in 1600s the Archduke Maximilian of Austria kept his horses here! However, for the last 400 years it serves as an Inn for the travelers to stay. Let's get in, shall we!"

"I've noticed that the small, family-owned hotels like these are very popular in Europe," said the cub.

"We've got the *Maximilian Suit*," the jaguar was guiding. "Look at the stuffed animal sculptures on the walls. This room is very comfortable, especially with this wood-burning fire place. Smells so good in here!"

"And... the furniture!" exclaimed the cub.

"These are all authentic pieces of the old Tirolean regions," said the jaguar.

"What I find most endearing in all of Europe, is the exuberant use of bells. Here, the bells ring almost every quarter of hour, summoning people for the religious, social or cultural events. They partake in the local life as much as the

people. I'm taking you now to a bell-foundry in Innsbrücke, a family-owned business site.

For nearly 415 years since 1599, the Grassmyar family masters signature grand-bells of a global fame. "

"The family resides in this simple, ordinary building," noticed the cub. "All the process of bell-making in conducted in here: the design, cast, forging and decoration. Let's see the *Frâu*."

An elegant Austrian lady met them in the foundry. "Alas, the famous bell from 1599 no longer exists," she explained, "but the one, from 1635, that rings everyday at noon time, is our product. It is not far away from here.. an hour ride."

"Who holds the family traditions today?" asked the cub.

"My husband gave it to our sons. My son Peter melts three tones more of copper into a bell than my husband! He makes the best bells ever! We run our 15th generation and so far, we have made 1,135 bells over 400 years. Each bell weighs about 4 tones and requires two weeks to cool. When it is ready, we lift it from the ground with the help of an indoor crane, then we peel it from the clay. From this moment on we are able to tell whether the bell has a good sound or not."

After testing the bell rings, the jaguar and the cub went to explore the town in the night.

"Innsbruck is the capital of the Tirolean region and it looks a kind of quiet city on surface. But you never know! Are you in a mood to see the Tirolean evening? This one is another family business: the Gyndolf family is a group of musicians and dancers. It entertains the tourists with a special folk-dancing involving ... guess what?

"Chopper, hammer, and pile!" the cub stretched his tail.

"Precisely so!   Now they are performing a traditional Tirolean dance called the *Woodchopper's Dance*. They also cook well and serve authentic meal."

"I see. Innsbrücke is much more than a resort for the Olympics," meowed the cub. "It is a place where the history alone deserves a visit.

I have comfortably parked my two sleds and now I would love a *'speck and goulash'* sandwich. No schnapps for me!" meowed the cub, grabbed a clawful of snow, and washed his whiskers.

Printed in Great Britain
by Amazon